Ready for Christmas?

Ready for Christmas?

Thinking through Advent

Peter Dainty

kevin mayhew

First published in 2005 by
KEVIN MAYHEW LTD
Buxhall, Stowmarket, Suffolk, IP14 3BW
E-mail: info@kevinmayhewltd.com
www.kevinmayhew.com

© 2005 Peter Dainty

The right of Peter Dainty to be identified as the author of this work has been asserted by him in accordance with the Copyright, Designs and Patents Act 1988.

No part of this publication may be reproduced, stored in a retrieval system, or transmitted, in any form or by any means, electronic, mechanical, photocopying, recording or otherwise, without the prior written permission of the publisher.

All rights reserved.

9 8 7 6 5 4 3 2 1 0

ISBN 1 84417 422 0
Catalogue No. 1500813

Cover illustration by Angela Palfrey
Cover design by Angela Selfe
Typeset by Fiona Connell-Finch

Printed and bound in Great Britain

Contents

Introduction

Week One LIGHT

Day 1	'Let there be light'	9
Day 2	The symbolism of light	11
Day 3	'O world invisible we view thee'	13
Day 4	Night and day	15
Day 5	Crying for the light	17
Day 6	Seeing the light	19
Day 7	Light from the Old Testament	21

Week Two HOPE

Day 8	The Old Testament hope	25
Day 9	The coming kingdom (Justice)	27
Day 10	The coming kingdom (Peace)	29
Day 11	Trouble ahead	31
Day 12	The kingdom now	33
Day 13	Surprise! Surprise!	35
Day 14	Changing the future	37

Week Three FAITHFUL SERVANTS

Day 15	Zechariah and Elizabeth	39
Day 16	In God's good time	41
Day 17	Mary	43
Day 18	The Magnificat	45
Day 19	Joseph	47
Day 20	Baby power	49
Day 21	Great expectations	51

Week Four JOHN THE BAPTIST

Day 22	The new Elijah?	53
Day 23	Repentance	55
Day 24	Baptism	57
Day 25	Judgement	59
Day 26	Ready?	61
Day 27	The fruit of repentance	63
Day 28	The One who is to come	65

Biblical Reference Index   67

Introduction

We spend an enormous amount of thought, emotion and energy in preparing for Christmas, but do we have time to prepare ourselves for Christ? This book is intended to help individuals and groups to do just that – to prepare inwardly and spiritually for the birth of Christ in the manger of the heart and the stable of the world.

Individuals could use this book as a daily reader based on the major themes of Advent (which aren't all the same as the themes of Christmas). There is a pause for thought at the end of each reading, which could lead into quiet prayer or silent waiting.

The book could also be used as a group course during the four weeks of Advent, with every member of the group using it daily and so preparing for the group meeting at the end of each week, when thoughts, feelings, actions and prayers could be shared. The final group meeting would have to be during the days after Christmas.

I know that time is at a premium in the weeks leading up to Christmas, but this only highlights the need for some time to be given to deeper things. Most Christians are uneasy about the way that the celebration of Christmas has evolved in the secular world, and how it is possible for many people to celebrate without thinking about Jesus Christ at all. For Christians this cannot be the way. How are we going to buck the trend and mark the Christian significance of Christmas, except by thinking and praying at a deeper level than the secular Christmas allows for? I hope this book will make some small contribution towards the re-Christening of Christmas.

PETER DAINTY

Bible quotations are from the NRSV except where indicated otherwise.

WEEK ONE
Light

DAY 1
'Let there be light'   Genesis 1:1-5 (2 Corinthians 4:8)

The first words attributed to God in the Bible are, 'Let there be light' (Genesis 1:3), and they could be understood as summing up God's purpose for creation – 'Let there be light.' The word 'light' could refer to physical light – the kind of light our eyes are sensitive to – the main source of which comes from the sun. The Big Bang theory suggests that the universe began with an explosion, though whether that explosion included a flash of light I couldn't be sure, not being much of a scientist.

But physical light does seem to have spread through the expanding universe from the beginning, with the constant creation of new galaxies and stars, so that on a clear night we can now see thousands of distant stars lighting up the sky and if we have a telescope we can detect billions more. In modern times artificial light has enabled us to extend our daily activities into the night, in a way which was almost impossible for our ancestors with their fires, torches, candles or oil lamps. Thomas Alva Edison succeeded in making the first electric light bulb in 1879, and when he died in 1931, at 10pm on the day of his funeral millions of Americans across the country switched off their electric lights for one minute in his memory and to remember what the world had been like before he lived.

So, 'Let there be light' may refer to the creation of physical light and its spread throughout the universe.

But it is also likely that 'light' is used in Genesis 1:3 in a symbolic sense, especially as the creation of the sun, moon and stars, which are the source of most of the natural light we can see with our eyes, doesn't take place in the Genesis story until the fifth day – *after* the creation of light in the beginning, and we know that throughout the Bible the word 'light' is used in both a physical and a metaphorical sense, just as it is in contemporary speech.

The Bible story takes us from the creation of light in Genesis, to the Holy City filled with the light of God's presence in the book of Revelation (21:23-24) as if to say that it is God's purpose to create a community which lives by the light of his glory in love, joy and peace. In between Genesis and Revelation we read the story of the coming of God's light into the world through a multitude of significant events in the history of his people.

But meanwhile we live somewhere between those two points. We have seen the coming of the light in Jesus Christ, but we still experience the darkness and wait for the fullness of the light at some point in the future, when God sums up all things in Christ. And it is during Advent that we look with hope and faith for the coming of God's light, wherever and whenever it may appear.

Pause for thought
'God is light and in him is no darkness at all' (1 John 1:5). Is this meant to be understood literally, metaphorically, or both? What does it mean?

DAY 2
The symbolism of light   Psalm 43:3a

There is more to reality than we can experience through our five senses. And there is more to light than meets the eye. That's why we use the word 'light' to try and describe some of the invisible dimensions of our existence. We talk about the light of consciousness, for instance, meaning that the mysterious gift of consciousness enables us to be aware of the world around us at a deeper level than the automatic response of our senses.

We also talk about the light of reason, because reason enables us to analyse the world around us so that we don't simply react to it, like plants or worms, we can use it and change it in complex ways. So words like 'consciousness', 'reason', 'knowledge' and 'intelligence' all have overlapping meanings, recognising that just as we are able to see with our eyes, so we are able to 'see' with our understanding too. We don't know how much conscious intelligence exists in the rest of the universe, but its existence on this planet is surely one of the greatest wonders of creation – a 'giant leap' from unconscious physical forces which don't 'know' what they're doing to conscious beings who do, even if their knowledge is limited.

There has been an enormous expansion of human knowledge over the last five thousand years and particularly in modern times. We don't always realise how much we owe to those scientists who have led the search for truth about the nature of the physical world and have made possible a vast improvement in the quality of life for millions of people. (Oh that these benefits were available to everyone.) This contemporary explosion of the light of knowledge has been quite remarkable. When Sir Isaac Newton, one of the founders of modern science, died, the poet Alexander Pope wrote an epitaph intended for him, which picked up the words of Genesis 1:5 –

> Nature and nature's laws lay hid in night;
> God said, 'Let Newton be!' and all was light.

Mind you, it is possible to take our admiration for scientific knowledge of the universe to the point where we regard it as more amazing than the universe itself – like the schoolboy who wrote in an essay that he didn't believe God created the world; he believed that science did. That is to ignore the fact that the universe already existed before the scientists got to know about it.

Pause for thought
Will scientists ever know everything?

Contents

Introduction

Week One LIGHT

Day 1	'Let there be light'	9
Day 2	The symbolism of light	11
Day 3	'O world invisible we view thee'	13
Day 4	Night and day	15
Day 5	Crying for the light	17
Day 6	Seeing the light	19
Day 7	Light from the Old Testament	21

Week Two HOPE

Day 8	The Old Testament hope	25
Day 9	The coming kingdom (Justice)	27
Day 10	The coming kingdom (Peace)	29
Day 11	Trouble ahead	31
Day 12	The kingdom now	33
Day 13	Surprise! Surprise!	35
Day 14	Changing the future	37

Week Three FAITHFUL SERVANTS

Day 15	Zechariah and Elizabeth	39
Day 16	In God's good time	41
Day 17	Mary	43
Day 18	The Magnificat	45
Day 19	Joseph	47
Day 20	Baby power	49
Day 21	Great expectations	51

Week Four JOHN THE BAPTIST

Day 22	The new Elijah?	53
Day 23	Repentance	55
Day 24	Baptism	57
Day 25	Judgement	59
Day 26	Ready?	61
Day 27	The fruit of repentance	63
Day 28	The One who is to come	65

Biblical Reference Index 67

Introduction

We spend an enormous amount of thought, emotion and energy in preparing for Christmas, but do we have time to prepare ourselves for Christ? This book is intended to help individuals and groups to do just that – to prepare inwardly and spiritually for the birth of Christ in the manger of the heart and the stable of the world.

Individuals could use this book as a daily reader based on the major themes of Advent (which aren't all the same as the themes of Christmas). There is a pause for thought at the end of each reading, which could lead into quiet prayer or silent waiting.

The book could also be used as a group course during the four weeks of Advent, with every member of the group using it daily and so preparing for the group meeting at the end of each week, when thoughts, feelings, actions and prayers could be shared. The final group meeting would have to be during the days after Christmas.

I know that time is at a premium in the weeks leading up to Christmas, but this only highlights the need for some time to be given to deeper things. Most Christians are uneasy about the way that the celebration of Christmas has evolved in the secular world, and how it is possible for many people to celebrate without thinking about Jesus Christ at all. For Christians this cannot be the way. How are we going to buck the trend and mark the Christian significance of Christmas, except by thinking and praying at a deeper level than the secular Christmas allows for? I hope this book will make some small contribution towards the re-Christening of Christmas.

PETER DAINTY

Bible quotations are from the NRSV except where indicated otherwise.

WEEK ONE
Light

DAY 1
'Let there be light' — Genesis 1:1-5 (2 Corinthians 4:8)

The first words attributed to God in the Bible are, 'Let there be light' (Genesis 1:3), and they could be understood as summing up God's purpose for creation – 'Let there be light.' The word 'light' could refer to physical light – the kind of light our eyes are sensitive to – the main source of which comes from the sun. The Big Bang theory suggests that the universe began with an explosion, though whether that explosion included a flash of light I couldn't be sure, not being much of a scientist.

But physical light does seem to have spread through the expanding universe from the beginning, with the constant creation of new galaxies and stars, so that on a clear night we can now see thousands of distant stars lighting up the sky and if we have a telescope we can detect billions more. In modern times artificial light has enabled us to extend our daily activities into the night, in a way which was almost impossible for our ancestors with their fires, torches, candles or oil lamps. Thomas Alva Edison succeeded in making the first electric light bulb in 1879, and when he died in 1931, at 10pm on the day of his funeral millions of Americans across the country switched off their electric lights for one minute in his memory and to remember what the world had been like before he lived.

So, 'Let there be light' may refer to the creation of physical light and its spread throughout the universe.

But it is also likely that 'light' is used in Genesis 1:3 in a symbolic sense, especially as the creation of the sun, moon and stars, which are the source of most of the natural light we can see with our eyes, doesn't take place in the Genesis story until the fifth day – *after* the creation of light in the beginning, and we know that throughout the Bible the word 'light' is used in both a physical and a metaphorical sense, just as it is in contemporary speech.

The Bible story takes us from the creation of light in Genesis, to the Holy City filled with the light of God's presence in the book of Revelation (21:23-24) as if to say that it is God's purpose to create a community which lives by the light of his glory in love, joy and peace. In between Genesis and Revelation we read the story of the coming of God's light into the world through a multitude of significant events in the history of his people.

But meanwhile we live somewhere between those two points. We have seen the coming of the light in Jesus Christ, but we still experience the darkness and wait for the fullness of the light at some point in the future, when God sums up all things in Christ. And it is during Advent that we look with hope and faith for the coming of God's light, wherever and whenever it may appear.

Pause for thought
'God is light and in him is no darkness at all' (1 John 1:5). Is this meant to be understood literally, metaphorically, or both? What does it mean?

DAY 2
The symbolism of light
Psalm 43:3a

There is more to reality than we can experience through our five senses. And there is more to light than meets the eye. That's why we use the word 'light' to try and describe some of the invisible dimensions of our existence. We talk about the light of consciousness, for instance, meaning that the mysterious gift of consciousness enables us to be aware of the world around us at a deeper level than the automatic response of our senses.

We also talk about the light of reason, because reason enables us to analyse the world around us so that we don't simply react to it, like plants or worms, we can use it and change it in complex ways. So words like 'consciousness', 'reason', 'knowledge' and 'intelligence' all have overlapping meanings, recognising that just as we are able to see with our eyes, so we are able to 'see' with our understanding too. We don't know how much conscious intelligence exists in the rest of the universe, but its existence on this planet is surely one of the greatest wonders of creation – a 'giant leap' from unconscious physical forces which don't 'know' what they're doing to conscious beings who do, even if their knowledge is limited.

There has been an enormous expansion of human knowledge over the last five thousand years and particularly in modern times. We don't always realise how much we owe to those scientists who have led the search for truth about the nature of the physical world and have made possible a vast improvement in the quality of life for millions of people. (Oh that these benefits were available to everyone.) This contemporary explosion of the light of knowledge has been quite remarkable. When Sir Isaac Newton, one of the founders of modern science, died, the poet Alexander Pope wrote an epitaph intended for him, which picked up the words of Genesis 1:5 –

> Nature and nature's laws lay hid in night;
> God said, 'Let Newton be!' and all was light.

Mind you, it is possible to take our admiration for scientific knowledge of the universe to the point where we regard it as more amazing than the universe itself – like the schoolboy who wrote in an essay that he didn't believe God created the world; he believed that science did. That is to ignore the fact that the universe already existed before the scientists got to know about it.

Pause for thought
Will scientists ever know everything?

DAY 7
Light from the Old Testament

Psalm 118:27a;
Psalm 119:105

The Old Testament tells the story of the way in which God's purposes were revealed to the people of Israel. It all happened in a different age and culture, but it is our story too and the Church has been a part of it for two thousand years (so far).

The light that dawned in Old Testament times was first of all belief in one God, who called Abram and his descendants away from the crudity and sometimes cruelty of polytheism and its associated fertility cults. Abraham's descendants also came to believe that God had high moral expectations of them, represented by the Law of Moses. The prophets reinforced these insights, because the people didn't always grasp them or live up to them (any more than we always live up to the teachings of Jesus) and it was only after they'd gone through the trauma of the conquest of their nation and the bitter experience of exile that their faith in one God and a deep reverence for his Law really took hold.

But after their tragic experiences many Jews became very wary of Gentiles and closed in on themselves to protect their community and their faith. This meant that the light of ethical monotheism, which God had given them to spread through the world, was treasured by them but not particularly shared with others. And that remained the situation at the time of the birth of Jesus. Jews and Gentiles were not exactly on good terms, and even in the early days of the Church, some Jewish Christians were unwilling to accept Gentiles into the Church unless they were first circumcised. Nevertheless, the more enlightened views of people like Paul and Barnabas were eventually accepted and the churches welcomed anyone who would believe in Christ as Lord and Saviour. So Christianity became a world-wide faith. But the ethical monotheism which forms the basis of that faith originated with the people of the Old Testament.

Belief in one creator God is, for many people, the most credible and satisfying explanation of the universe. Scientific theories about creation can only tell us how the universe came into being and developed into its present state over billions of years; they can't tell us whether the universe has any purpose, because purpose implies a Purposer, and that's a personal concept. Science can only describe the universe in impersonal terms, as the interaction between various forces. Johann Kepler was one of the founders of modern science in the seventeenth century, who believed that the universe was created by God. But he had an atheist friend who tried to persuade him that the universe came into being of itself, by mechanical methods. So Kepler constructed a model of the solar system showing the planets moving round the sun and invited his friend to see it. His friend was very impressed by the model and said to Kepler: 'It's marvellous! Who made it?' Kepler answered: 'Nobody made it. It made itself,' to which his friend said, 'Nonsense! Somebody must have made it.' Kepler remarked, 'My friend, you think this little toy could not have made itself, but it is only a poor imitation of the world which *you* claim *did* make itself. *That's* nonsense!' Now whatever you make of Kepler's argument, the fact is that no philosopher or scientist has been able to replace the idea of God as creator with an idea which is more positive or inspiring. And we got that idea from the Old Testament.

It was H. G. Wells who said that 'the religion of the atheist has a god-shaped blank at its heart,' and he might have added – the atheist doesn't know how to fill it.

We also owe our fundamental ideas of right and wrong to the Old Testament – justice, mercy, love for our neighbour, concern for the poor and vulnerable – though these ideas were developed even further by Jesus. Nowadays we like to think that we can reinvent morality, but if we dismantle everything that we owe to the past we shall probably find that we have dismantled society itself, and everything will fall into chaos.

Twentieth-century atheist, Bertrand Russell, said that he didn't know where moral ideas came from. He believed cruelty was wrong, but he was unable to explain why. Christians, Jews and Muslims believe that moral ideals are essentially God-given, and this is symbolised for us in the Old Testament by the story of

Moses receiving the Ten Commandments from God on Mount Sinai. If there are no moral absolutes, anything goes, and if anything goes, ultimately everything goes.

So the light of faith and morality, which has come to us from the Old Testament, is essential if we are to find our way through the darkness.

Pause for thought
How important to you is belief in one good God who is the creator of the universe?

WEEK TWO
Hope

DAY 8
The Old Testament hope
Jeremiah 29:11

It took a long time for the people of Israel to get a firm hold of the idea of one God, and they kept reverting to the fertility cults of Canaan. They also took a long time to take God's Law seriously and the prophets had to remind them of their calling over and over again. But when their nation was destroyed (including the city of Jerusalem and the Temple) and many of them were carried off into exile in Babylonia, just as the prophets had foretold, they realised that they needed to return to the faith of their ancestors if they were going to survive as a people. They kept their religious practices alive in exile (except for sacrifice, which could only take place in the Temple) by meeting in synagogues for prayer and the study of the Scriptures. They especially revered the Torah, the first five books of our present Bible, recording the Law of Moses. Psalm 119 gives us an idea of how important the Law became to the Jewish people (e.g. see verses 72, 103 and 105).

The Jews in exile also kept *hope* alive. Helped by the teaching of the prophets, they were encouraged to believe that they would return one day to their beloved Jerusalem, which they began to do in 538 BC, because the Babylonian Empire had fallen to the armies of Cyrus of Persia.

But of special importance was the Jewish hope that the kingdom of David would eventually be restored, ruled over by one of his descendants. Jerusalem would then become the centre of the world's attention and the Gentiles would come to Israel bearing tributes and seeking to worship Israel's God. This golden age to come would see the establishment of an ideal Davidic kingdom of justice and peace, and it is referred to in several of the Advent lectionary passages (e.g. 2 Samuel 7:1-11; Psalm 72:1-7, 18-19; Psalm 89:1-4, 19-26; Isaiah 2:1-5; Isaiah 11:1-10 and Micah

5:1-5a to which we might add Isaiah 9:2-7, one of the readings for Christmas Day).

It was an ideal which Luke refers to in his account of the birth of Jesus (e.g. 1:32-33, 69) and Mary's song (The Magnificat – Luke 1:46-55) depicts a time of justice similar to that looked forward to in the Old Testament (for instance, compare Luke 1:50-54 with Psalm 72:1-4, 13-14; and compare the end of Zechariah's song in Luke 1:79 with Isaiah's words in Isaiah 9:2).

The unknown prophet whose writings are included with the prophecies of Isaiah speaks not of a coming King, but of a Servant of the Lord, called by God to be 'a light to the nations': 'It is too light a thing that you should be my servant to raise up the tribes of Jacob and to restore the survivors of Israel; I will give you as a light to the nations (Gentiles), that my salvation may reach to the end of the earth' (Isaiah 49:6). These words are echoed by Luke in the prayer of Simeon (Luke 2:32); and Matthew's story of the Wise Men's visit to Bethlehem also reflects these Old Testament hopes (see Psalm 72:10-11).

The kingdom of God is therefore a hope, not only for the Jews, but for all humankind.

Pause for thought
To what extent were Old Testament hopes fulfilled by Jesus?

DAY 9
The coming kingdom (Justice)   Amos 5:24

Those Old Testament hopes were long ago. What have they got to do with us in the twenty-first century? The relevance of these ancient prophecies lies in our own hopes for the rule of justice and peace in the world, encapsulated in one of the ideas most talked about by Jesus in his teaching – the idea of the kingdom of God in which God's will is done here on earth as it is in heaven.

Most of us would want to pay at least lip service to the ideal of a world full of justice and peace and there are those who are devoting their energies towards that end, in organisations such as Christian Aid, Cafod, Tear Fund, Fair Trade, Oxfam, and the United Nations as well as in movements such as 'Make Poverty History'. Others work in the churches and social services, the diplomatic service, the political parties, the legal profession and even in business and financial institutions with a vision of a better world in their eyes. We can only admire them and try to support their efforts and initiatives as best we can.

But how realistic are such hopes and ideals? Will we ever rid the world of poverty, for instance? Even Jesus said, 'You always have the poor with you' (Matthew 26:11), and many have used those words as an excuse to do nothing about eradicating poverty, though helping the poor by means of almsgiving has always been a prominent feature of religious life (see Deuteronomy 15:11). That is very different, however, from changing the system so that poverty is removed altogether. But is it possible?

The question we should really be asking ourselves about this is: 'Does God really want us to establish justice on earth?' If the answer is 'Yes, of course,' then that implies the abolition of poverty, because poverty is the biggest injustice in the world today, and we can see its dreadful consequences in many places. Moreover, we can see the dreadful effects of poverty everywhere, because it nurtures resentment, anger, hatred and violence. The present surge in world-wide terrorism has been fuelled at least to some extent by the huge and unjust gap between the rich and poor on an international scale. The rich world's answer to terrorism seems to be to spend billions on measures to fight against it, but to be unenthusiastic when it comes to dealing with the injustices which cause terrorism – including poverty.

The rich world undoubtedly profits from the resources available in the poorer countries in the form of material resources, cheap labour and expanding markets, but it cannot always isolate itself from some of the more difficult side effects of poverty – the spread of diseases, the cost of dealing with the after effects of disasters of one kind or another, and the need to control the rising tide of economic migration.

The fact that it is in the rich world's own interest to deal seriously with the issue of poverty should give us hope that it will be possible to 'make poverty history'.

In February 2005, Nelson Mandela addressed a meeting of twenty thousand 'Make Poverty History' campaigners in Trafalgar Square. He said, 'Like slavery and apartheid, poverty is not natural. It is man-made and it can be overcome and eradicated by the actions of human beings. Overcoming poverty is an act of justice.' He also said that he had recently announced his retirement from public life and shouldn't really be there in Trafalgar Square. 'However,' he said, none of us can truly rest 'as long as poverty, injustice and gross inequality persist in our world.' Those words reminded me of the description of the Servant of the Lord in Isaiah 42:4, 'He will not grow faint or be crushed until he has established justice in the earth.' That won't be easy, by any means, but with the Lord, nothing is impossible (see Matthew 19:26).

Pause for thought
Do you really think it will be possible to eradicate poverty from the earth?

DAY 10
The coming kingdom (Peace) Micah 4:3

There can be no lasting peace without justice, though it must be a justice tempered by mercy, forgiveness, tolerance and patience on all sides. However, we need to ask the same questions about the possibility of eradicating war as a means of trying solve problems as we have asked about the possibility of eradicating poverty.

Will we ever rid the world of war? It seems like an impossible dream, and that there will *always* be 'wars and rumours of wars' (Matthew 24:6). Resort to violence and retaliation seems to be an automatic response of human nature, resulting in a seemingly endless 'spiral of violence' as Helder Camara described it.

In an issue of the *Primitive Methodist Magazine* in 1897 there was an article on war and peace which began: 'In the evolution of human society, and as a result of the play of Christian forces, it is gratifying to note a growing dislike of war and bloodshed and an increasing demand for righteousness, brotherhood and peace among the nations of the earth.' But seventeen years later those nations embarked on one of the bloodiest wars in history.

In his *Short History of the World*, published in 1926, H. G. Wells wrote, 'Can anyone doubt that presently our race will achieve unity and peace.' Only a few years later, the so-called Aryan Race, in the guise of Nazism, launched Germany into the Holocaust and the rest of the world into another bloodbath. In despair H. G. Wells replaced the last chapter of his book with one entitled, 'Mind at the End of its Tether' (1946), declaring that *Homo Sapiens* in his present form was played out and would have to give place to some other animal.

It was Arthur Koestler who said that the most important date in human history was 6 August 1945, when the first atom bomb was dropped on Hiroshima. Since that date, he said, the extinction of the whole human race has become an ever-present possibility.

But we go on hoping for peace, perhaps inspired by the hopes of those Old Testament prophets, whose visions still stir our cynical hearts (e.g. Isaiah 2:4). We keep on hoping, just as the prophets kept on hoping, because we believe that those visions and hopes come from God.

And God is always working his purposes out, even though that work is often hidden from our eyes. It was a seven-year-old boy who said, 'I have been praying to God for over a year now to stop the fighting and wars, but he hasn't done anything about it – yet.' I like that word 'yet', because it showed that the boy's hope was still alive. Some of us have been praying for peace in the world for much longer than that and we know that it isn't time to give up praying yet, because we have already seen signs of God at work in several places; one of the most dramatic was the end of the Cold War between east and west.

In 1967, this prayer was offered during a ceremony to launch a Polaris nuclear submarine, part of the west's military deterrent against the nuclear threat from the Communist east. The chaplain held up a cross and prayed, 'Lord, here is your cross; you must bear it alone. It is too hard for us; we need other defences. It is too simple; we must have our own strategies. We know all the arguments; we have never heard yours. Lord, argue with us; show us new ways. Get us out of the situation we've landed ourselves in, for your world's sake.'

Was the end of the Cold War God's answer to that prayer? Maybe. But the threat of nuclear extinction still remains, unless we can find ways of abolishing war altogether.

Pause for thought
How would you answer someone who said that praying for peace was a waste of time?

DAY 11
Trouble ahead   Acts 14:22

One of the most difficult aspects of Advent is the apocalyptic theme of the end of the world and the second coming of Jesus Christ. The compilers of the lectionary have tried to protect us from the most demanding passages simply by omitting or reducing them. For instance, we are not invited to read the whole of Matthew 24 or Mark 13, but only a short passage from each. Nor is there any reference to the Book of Revelation. This may be a deliberate policy to avoid frightening people too much, or it may be an attempt to discourage irrational speculation about the future by people with overheated imaginations. I'm not sure which.

On the other hand, we have to be realistic and avoid looking into the future through rose-tinted spectacles. One message that comes across clearly from these passages (Luke 21:25-36 is the nearest we get to them in the lectionary) is that easy optimism is not an option for Christians. The kingdom of God won't be established on earth without a great deal of blood, sweat and tears along the way. Given human nature and even the nature of the physical world, that will include wars, revolutions, persecutions, earthquakes, famines, plagues, 'signs in the sun, the moon, and the stars, and on the earth distress among nations confused by the roaring of the sea and the waves' (Luke 21:9, 11-12, 25).

Such prophecies are a happy hunting ground for all those who want to see every war and earthquake as a sign that the end of the world is near. (Maybe such people are among the false messiahs and false prophets mentioned in Mark 13:22 and Matthew 24:24.) On the other hand, every war and earthquake is, in a sense, a sign of the end of the world, because it illustrates the precarious nature of our civilisation and our lives on this planet.

Many of these prophecies are made more confusing because they are mixed up with prophecies of the destruction of Jerusalem by the Romans, which took place in AD 70. If we look more closely at the Scriptures we will see that many of these things will happen, 'but the end is not yet' (Matthew 24:6; also verse 7, and Mark 13:7-8 as well as Luke 21:9).

But one thing is clear; the prophecies are aimed at encouraging those who look forward to the coming kingdom to cling on to hope and faith no matter what happens, because, however dreadful things get, 'the one who endures to the end will be saved' (Matthew 24:13; Mark 13:13b), and there is nothing in the whole creation which can separate us from the love of God in Christ Jesus our Lord (Romans 8:38-39).

This raises another problem for us, because many of us – perhaps all who are alive today – will not be around when 'the end' comes. In fact no one knows when the end will take place, except the Father – not even the Son or the angels (Mark 13:32). So, like all those who lived before us, the best we can do is to remain faithful by looking for the kingdom all our days and passing on our hope to future generations.

This is well illustrated by a story from New England in the eighteenth century, when there was a widespread belief that the end of the world was imminent. One day at noon the sky turned very black over the State capital when the house of representatives was in session. Many of the members thought that Judgement Day had arrived and they left their seats in a panic, heading towards the doors. The Speaker of the House, Colonel Davenport, rose to his feet and calmly addressed the members with these words: 'Gentlemen,' he said, 'either the Day of Judgement *has* arrived, or it has not. If it has not, there is no cause for alarm. If it has arrived, then I for one desire to be found by the Lord faithfully doing my duty. Gentlemen, let the candles be lit, and let us proceed with the business of the House.'

As Jesus said, 'Blessed is that slave whom his master will find at work when he arrives' (Matthew 24:46).

Pause for thought
What should our Christian response be to the idea of the end of the world?

DAY 12
The kingdom now
Mark 1:15

Jesus' teaching about the kingdom of God is that it is already here. According to Mark 1:15, when Jesus began his preaching ministry in Galilee, he said, 'The time is fulfilled, and the kingdom of God has come near (or 'is at hand'); repent, and believe in the good news.' Jesus saw himself and his ministry as signs that the kingdom had come already (Luke 11:20).

This may seem to contradict the idea that the kingdom will come in the future on God's appointed day, but if we can regard the kingdom of God as the rule of God we shall realise that both ideas are true. We can enter into God's kingdom now by submitting ourselves to his rule and allowing his will to work itself out in our lives, but we can also look forward to the day when God's rule is as fully established on earth as it is in heaven.

Frederick Luke Wiseman was a leading figure in the Methodist Church between the wars. As a teenage boy he was very moved by a sermon preached by his grandfather. After the service the boy asked his grandfather when the whole world would accept Jesus Christ. His grandfather replied, 'I don't know when the whole world will accept him, but the whole world cannot accept him until Frederick Luke Wiseman has.'

It's exactly the same with the kingdom of God. When will the kingdom of God be universally established? The answer is that it cannot be universally established unless it is established in me.

Or we could look at it from another angle. Jesus once said, 'The kingdom of God has come near to you' (Luke 10:9). There's an old story from Norfolk about the pedlar of Swaffham, John Chapman. He was an idle fellow who dreamed of finding gold, and one night he was told in a dream that if he went and stood on London Bridge he would find the gold. So he tramped off to London and stood on London Bridge for three days – but found nothing. As he was about to set off back to Swaffham, bitterly disappointed, a shopkeeper asked him why he had been standing there. The pedlar told him about his dream, and the shopkeeper laughed and said,

'I had a dream like that, and it told me to go to a pedlar's house in Swaffham and I would find gold buried under the roots of a tree in the back garden, but I took no notice of it.' The pedlar rushed back home and dug under the tree in his garden, and there found the gold he'd been looking for.

Perhaps John Chapman had to go to London Bridge before he discovered that there was gold in his own back garden. And perhaps we have to go on many spiritual adventures in search of the kingdom of God before we find that it is buried right there 'within us' in our own hearts, or 'among us' in our own community. For God is present everywhere, just waiting for us to respond to his invitation to enter into his kingdom here and now. We needn't wait till the 'end of the world' before we are able to share justice and peace with our neighbours.

God simply calls us to let the light that is within us shine out into the world (Matthew 5:14-16), or as Paul put it, 'The night is far gone, the day is near. Let us then lay aside the works of darkness and put on the armour of light' (Romans 13:12).

Pause for thought
Is there anything to prevent us from entering the kingdom of God right here and now?

DAY 13
Surprise! Surprise!   Isaiah 43:18-19a

No one can predict the future with any degree of accuracy, except, perhaps in the very short term, and even then we can get it wrong. Weather forecasters, with the aid of sophisticated satellites and computers, aren't always accurate in their day-to-day forecasts, and much less so in the longer term. That is because the weather system is so complex, and even a tiny change in air pressure or wind direction can have a huge knock-on effect. History is very complex too and that makes predictions of the future almost impossible. We base our predictions on what we know from the past, plus a little bit of imagination (sometimes a lot of imagination).

That's why the future tends to be full of surprises which nobody could have foreseen, except in the most general terms. If anyone had foreseen how television would work in the eighteenth century they would have been able to invent it there and then. That is why prophecies don't always make sense to us, because they are trying to picture something that has never happened before, and they can only do it by using the ideas which are already familiar to them and dressing them up a bit.

So when we read about 'the Son of Man coming in a cloud with power and great glory' (Luke 21:27), we don't know what to make of it. We may know that Jesus often called himself the Son of Man, though we don't know exactly what he meant by that. He may have seen himself as a representative human being, and he may also have been referring to the prophecy in Daniel 7:13-15 which describes 'one like a human being' receiving 'dominion and glory and kingship' from 'the Ancient One' (i.e. God), enabling him to rule over all the nations as their everlasting king. This is obviously a grandiose version of the messianic hope. It is an image from the distant past which today we probably find difficult to understand. 'Coming in a cloud with power and great glory' may even make us think of an invasion from outer space.

But what the prophecy is trying to express, when it is used in the New Testament, is the belief that Christ will ultimately rule the world. The imagery is in stark contrast with the baby lying in a manger in Bethlehem and the Nazarene preacher hanging on a cross outside the walls of Jerusalem, but that is exactly why it is so remarkable. The early Christians knew all about world rulers and the ever-present power of Rome, yet they also believed that Christ and his way would outlast all earthly empires, however powerful they seem to be.

Jesus used a simple image to describe this belief – the image of the house built on sand and the house built on rock (Matthew 7:24-27) – an image that we can easily understand. It is saying that any life or society based on anything less than the principles of love, forgiveness, generosity, honesty and faith revealed in the life and teaching of Jesus is bound to collapse, whereas lives built on those principles will survive any storm. It is a great faith and a great hope.

But whether the prophecies which describe this faith will turn out to be literally true is impossible for us to know. Most of the other prophecies of the coming of the Messiah were proved to be inaccurate, because when the Messiah actually arrived he was not a King or a military warrior, but a working man from Nazareth with no authority but the authority of his life and teaching; and with no intention of driving out the Romans, but of welcoming the outcasts into his 'kingdom' of love.

Pause for thought
Can you think of any surprises, either in your own life, or in human history?

DAY 14
Changing the future
Romans 12:17, 21

It's impossible to change the past, but it's always possible to change the future, and the opportunity to do so comes to us every day.

Of course, people can rewrite history, and often do so. But the truth of what happened in the past is still true no matter how much we may gloss it over. We can also forgive the wrongs of the past, but those wrongs still happened just the same. By forgiving them we aren't changing the past, but the future; preventing the bitterness of those wrongs from poisoning what lies ahead.

So what we do today undoubtedly affects the shape of the future. Things could have been worse, or better, if we had acted differently. That is why Frank Capra's *It's a Wonderful Life* is one of the most popular films ever made. It tells how George Bailey, faced with bankruptcy and filled with despair as his world seems to be collapsing around him, is on the point of committing suicide. But an angel called Clarence is sent to help him. Clarence points out all the good things George has done in his life and shows him what the small town where he lives would have been like if he'd never lived – a sleazy, squalid place run by crooks and full of debt, violence and misery. In the end he returns to his family and is saved from bankruptcy by gifts of money from his friends – a very happy ending.

We may not think that our own actions could have such dramatic effects on the community where we live, let alone on the wider world beyond, but we forget the power of the knock-on effect I mentioned yesterday, which makes weather forecasting so difficult. It may seem trite to say it, but it's true nevertheless, that smiles and laughter, kindness and encouragement, generosity and forgiveness are powerfully infectious, and can make all the difference to the people we meet, and to ourselves too. Of course, grumpy faces, nasty attitudes, hurtful words, meanness and hate also have a powerful effect. That is why it is so important that we take care over our words and attitudes in daily life. By our choices we have the ability to change the future for better or for worse.

Some people set out deliberately to change the future by inventing or discovering something new, or by devoting their lives to a cause. This too can have good or bad effects, perhaps unforeseen by the person concerned. But the surest way of changing the future for the better is by living a good life today, especially when faced with wrong. It often takes great courage to do this, but it can bear surprising fruit in the long run.

The people of Fiji today are generally friendly and peace loving, but in the nineteenth century they were ruled over by a fierce cannibal chief, called Thakombau. He used to quell any opposition by battering his opponents to death with his wooden war clubs, and then he'd have the bodies prepared to be eaten at a cannibal feast. Mary and James Calvert went to Fiji from England as missionaries in 1838. While they were there chief Thakombau ordered fifteen girls to be killed and their bodies prepared for a feast. Plucking up courage Mary Calvert went to see the chief and managed to persuade him to release five of the girls. Later Thakombau was taken seriously ill (it must have been something he ate!) and his people began to think they might be rid of him. But again, Mary Calvert went to see him, and this time she nursed him back to health. Under her good influence he became a changed man, and at a special ceremony he handed over his war clubs to the missionaries, as a sign that the islands would no longer be ruled by violence, but by Jesus Christ.

People with faith and courage can make all the difference in situations ruled by fear and hate, and so change the future for the better.

Pause for thought

Do you know of any situation which has been changed for the better by the words or actions of good people?

Think about any things you've said or done in the past, or failed to say or do, which you now regret. Ask God for forgiveness, and the grace to learn from your mistakes.

WEEK THREE
Faithful Servants

DAY 15
Zechariah and Elizabeth Luke 1:5-25, 39-45, 57-80

The story of Zechariah (Zacharias in Greek) and Elizabeth and the birth of John the Baptist, as told by Luke, serves as a link between the Old Testament and the New. We are familiar with the way that childless couples played a key role in God's purposes from the stories of Sarah and Abraham and the birth of Esau (Genesis 18:1-15; 21:1-8), and Hannah and Elkanah and the birth of Samuel (1 Samuel 1). The birth of Esau enabled the line of Abraham's descendants to continue, and God's promises to him to be fulfilled; and the birth of Samuel opened the way for the era of prophets and kings in Israel's history. The birth of John to Elizabeth and Zechariah is similarly a crucial step in God's plans for the coming of the Messiah.

It was four hundred years since the last prophet in the Old Testament, Malachi, recorded the Lord's words to his people, and almost the last words of the Lord recorded by Malachi are, 'Lo, I will send you the prophet Elijah before the great and terrible day of the Lord comes' (Malachi 4:5).

Well, Elijah was a long time coming, and some may have thought that the Lord had forgotten his promise, as their fathers had thought during the Babylonian exile. Plaintive cries such as 'How long, O Lord? Will you hide yourself for ever?' (Psalm 89:46) are frequent in the Psalms, and in more recent times such feelings of despair were often expressed during the Holocaust of the 1930s and 1940s. Sometimes we may feel the same way in our own lives. Where is God when we need him? Why does he seem to hide himself in times of greatest distress? Has he forgotten us? At such times, we can either give up on God altogether, or just keep treading the path of faith and duty until the Lord reveals himself.

Zechariah and Elizabeth were treading the path of faith and

duty when we are introduced to them by Luke. Zechariah and his wife, Elizabeth, 'were righteous before God, living blamelessly according to all the commandments and regulations of the Lord' (Luke 1:6). And Zechariah was fulfilling his priestly duties in the temple, when suddenly, 'out of the blue' you might say, he had a vision of the messenger (angel) of the Lord. At long last God's silence was broken and the angel quoted from Malachi 4:5-6 to make this clear (Luke 1:17). The time was now right for the next stage in God's ancient plan and Zechariah and his wife had an important part to play in it through the unexpected birth of a son in their old age – a son who would be the new Elijah, come 'to make ready a people prepared for the Lord' (Luke 1:17b). Ironically, the sign given to Zechariah to show him that the Lord had spoken through the angel was that he himself was unable to speak, or hear, till after the birth of his son. The end of the long silence of God was thus marked by the shorter silence of Zechariah. He was speechless – which was a fitting response to the word of the Lord.

The meaning of his name is also fitting – Zechariah means 'the Lord remembers' (or 'has remembered'). And Elizabeth means 'the oath of God'. Those meanings illustrate one of the basic aspects of their story, that God does not forget his promises. It was the angel Gabriel who announced the name of their son (Luke 1:13b), and Elizabeth and Zechariah didn't forget it when they were under pressure to call their baby Zechariah after his father. No – he was to be called John, which means, 'the grace of God'. And that is just what they had experienced through those mysterious events, while many others were to experience the same grace through the even more remarkable events that lay ahead.

The story of Zechariah and Elizabeth also shows us that God does not forget us in old age, but can use us still to serve his purposes.

Pause for thought
How do you react when God seems to be silent?

DAY 16
In God's good time
2 Peter 3:9

We can't understand God's way of working, because we don't know enough. Only God knows when the time is right. We may think he is slow, but that is because we are too ignorant and too impatient. The second letter of Peter reminds us that 'the Lord is not slow about his promise, as some think of slowness' (2 Peter 3:9), and since 'one day is like a thousand years' to him 'and a thousand years are like one day' (2 Peter 3:8), it's obvious that God's understanding of time is very different from ours.

Some have tried to suggest why God waited until the days of the Roman Empire before sending the Messiah. They point out that those were days of relative peace and political stability in the Mediterranean world. There was a universal language (Koiné Greek) and established routes for travel and communication. These things would make it easy for the gospel (good news) to be spread by the followers of Christ. They may be right, but we can't always see things clearly enough at the time to be sure. We just have to trust and obey, and leave the planning and timing to God.

It was in 1948 that the idea of building a modern hospice began to germinate in the mind of Cicely Saunders, but it wasn't until 1959 that she felt God nudging her to do something about it, as she read her daily Bible passage and the words: 'Commit thy way unto the Lord; trust also in him; and he shall bring it to pass' (Psalm 37:5 AV). Four years later she had found some suitable land for building the hospice, but was having difficulty getting grants for the work. On 7 February 1963 her daily reading included the words, 'Thou shalt bless the Lord thy God for the good land he hath given thee' (Deuteronomy 8:10 AV), and that same evening she received a call from the King Edward's Hospital Fund telling her she could have the money she'd applied for. So St Christopher's Hospice was built – the first of many more to follow. God worked through Cicely Saunders, but always at his own pace.

It is up to us to plant the seeds of God's kingdom, but it is God who gives the growth (see 1 Corinthians 3:5-9). Seeds don't grow very quickly, and they can lie dormant until the right conditions come along. But only God knows when that is. That's why Paul urged Timothy to preach the word 'in season and out of season' (2 Timothy 4:2 AV), then there would always be some planted seed ready to grow when the time was right.

One thing we *can* be sure of is that God never forgets us, however long the time scale of his purposes. According to the Bible, the only thing God ever forgets is our sins (Jeremiah 31:34; Isaiah 43:25) and that's surely a blessing.

The unnamed prophet of the exile said that God is less likely to forget Zion than a woman is to forget the child at her breast (Isaiah 49:15); and God remembered his people in exile, just as he had remembered them in Egyptian slavery. From our point of view he often seems to take his time, but all he asks his servants to do is trust and obey, and leave the rest to him.

Pause for thought
Have you ever got impatient with God's apparent slowness to act? Was your impatience justified?

DAY 17
Mary
Luke 1:26-38

In contrast with the announcement of the birth of John the Baptist, which came to an elderly priest in the Temple in Jerusalem, the announcement of the birth of Jesus came to a young girl in Nazareth in Galilee. Jerusalem was at the heart of the Jewish world; Galilee bordered on Gentile lands. The Temple was regarded as the dwelling place of God and the holy place of sacrificial worship; Mary's house in Nazareth was an ordinary home. Such is the unpredictability of God. His messages can come to us anywhere, whether we are old or young.

In July 1945 Leonard Cheshire was on leave for a few days in London, and went one evening to a pub in Mayfair to celebrate with a few colleagues. The conversation got around to religion and Cheshire tried to change the subject with some vague comment equating God with conscience. Somebody retorted: 'You're talking nonsense. God is a person and you know it.' And suddenly Cheshire did know it. He knew it with an absolute certainty, and that moment in a Mayfair pub proved to be the turning point in his religious life. God had spoken to him at an unexpected time and in an unexpected place.

The angelic messages came to both Mary and Zechariah at an unexpected time. Both of them were disturbed by their experience, and questioned the credibility of what they were being told, but neither of them laughed it off as a mental aberration. They both accepted the message and its consequences. Mary's response was positive and direct: 'Here am I, the servant of the Lord; let it be with me according to your word' (Luke 1:38). It reminds us of Isaiah's response to his vision of God in the Temple (Isaiah 6:8). Zechariah needed a bit more convincing than Mary, but he got the message in the end. The essential human ingredients in both these stories were faith and obedience.

When God confronts us, the place and time don't matter, but faith is essential. God may have tried to get through to many people over the centuries, but their lack of faith has prevented him from being able to do much through them. That is why Jesus was always looking for faith in the people he met, and he was delighted when he found it (e.g. Matthew 8:10), but disappointed when he didn't (e.g. Matthew 17:17). Matthew tells us that Jesus was unable to do many mighty works in his home town 'because of their unbelief' (Matthew 13:58). On the other hand Jesus told his disciples that if they had faith the size of a mustard seed they could move mountains (Matthew 17:20).

I don't think it's too strong to say that by our faith we give permission for God to act. He will not overrule our free will, but would rather wait for faith to give him the go-ahead, because we can then share in the working out of his purposes. By her faith, Mary gave permission for God to become incarnate in the world. He wouldn't (or couldn't?) do it without her. By giving birth, Mary brought God into the world. It sounds a startling thought, but when you think about it, it is when someone hears, believes and obeys the Word of the Lord, that the Word actually becomes flesh.

Pause for thought
Think of different ways in which God speaks to us.

DAY 18
The Magnificat   Luke 1:46-55

We are told these days that the mood of a mother during pregnancy can affect the development of the child in the womb – if her mood is bitter, anxious, angry, tense or sad, this can have a negative influence on the growing child; peace of mind, relaxation, cheerfulness, goodwill and hope can have a positive influence.

Certain actions can also affect the unborn child – smoking, drinking and violent activity are obvious examples of things which might be bad for the baby. Gentle singing, rocking or speaking may have a beneficial effect.

Mary exclaimed this famous song of rejoicing, praise and hope. It has often been sung in the Church's worship, though whether Mary sang it or said it we don't really know, but the words reflect her mood of joy because of the privilege of being chosen to give birth to this special child. The words of the Magnificat echo the prayer of Hannah when she brought her son Samuel to the Temple to 'lend' him to the Lord (1 Samuel 2:1-10).

Like Hannah, Mary links the birth of her son to the rebirth of her people in line with God's justice – the proud and mighty are brought low, the poor and hungry are raised up, and Israel becomes the kind of community God always hoped it would be. What effect, I wonder, did Mary's 'song' have on her embryo son? We can't be sure, but it's interesting to note that when Jesus began his mission in Galilee, preaching that the kingdom of God was at hand, he went to the synagogue in Nazareth and stood up to read from the book of the prophet Isaiah, choosing a passage (61:1-2a) predicting similar signs of social rebirth. And he followed up his reading by stating: 'Today this scripture has been fulfilled in your hearing' (Luke 4:21).

It's probably fanciful to think that Jesus heard that song while he was in his mother's womb, and even more fanciful to think that he understood it. But it's reasonable to think that if his mother had that kind of faith in God and a vision of his kingdom in her heart, she passed them on to Jesus when he was a growing boy. We do know that Jesus grew up to have a deep understanding of the Jewish religion, which he showed when he visited the temple at the age of twelve, and it is more than likely that he learned that not only from the synagogue school but from the influence and encouragement of his parents.

That's why the neglect of religious education in the home today is such a worrying development in modern society. When faith in God and a vision of his kingdom disappear from the land we shall be in serious trouble, for 'where there is no vision, the people perish' (Proverbs 29:18 AV).

When Hannah took her boy Samuel to the Temple to grow up 'in the presence of the Lord' (1 Samuel 2:21b), we are told that 'the word of the Lord was rare in those days; visions were not widespread' (1 Samuel 3:1), in fact the two sons of Eli, the High Priest, were scoundrels who had no regard for the Lord and even blasphemed against him (1 Samuel 2:12; 3:13). So the High Priest's own sons were out of his control and he had failed to pass on to them his own devotion to God. But at least he was able to encourage Samuel in the faith.

Mary, on the other hand, had a blameless record in this respect, and brought up Jesus so that he 'increased in wisdom and in years, and in divine and human favour' (Luke 2:52).

Pause for thought
Did our parents pass on their faith to us? How can we pass on our faith to our own children?

DAY 19
Joseph
Matthew 1:18-25

Although Joseph is overshadowed by Mary in the Bible accounts, he still plays an important part in the story. First, and in spite of the virgin birth, it was through Joseph, and not through Mary, that Jesus was descended from David. Both Matthew and Luke provide family trees which make this clear (Matthew 1:1-16 and Luke 3:23-38). Matthew describes Joseph as 'son of David' (Matthew 1:20) and Luke tells how it was because Joseph was of the house and family of David that he and Mary went to Bethlehem to be registered (Luke 2:4), the result being that Jesus was born in the city of David.

Secondly, Joseph was a 'righteous' man who respected the Law of Israel. When he found out that his fiancée was pregnant he decided to break off their engagement, but to do it discreetly so that Mary wasn't exposed to public disgrace (Matthew 1:19). But when he found out the reason for her pregnancy he didn't hesitate to marry her. After Jesus was born Joseph and Mary followed the requirements of the Law, by having their baby circumcised (Luke 2:21), and later they took him to the Temple in Jerusalem to present him to the Lord, offering a sacrifice of two turtle doves and two young pigeons as the Law required (Luke 2:22-24). Luke also tells us that Joseph and Mary went to Jerusalem for the Passover Festival every year (Luke 2:41). No doubt their devotion to the Law of Moses and regular visits to the Temple impressed themselves on the mind of Jesus, so that he himself grew up to love Jerusalem and the Temple and to be a regular attender at the synagogue (Luke 4:16; 19:41-46). Such is the powerful influence of parental example.

Thirdly, Joseph was a practical man. Matthew tells us that he was a carpenter (Matthew 13:55) and therefore had a skill which would not only be of service to the community, but would also enable him to provide for his family. No doubt it was a skill which he was able to use while the family were in Bethlehem, and when they lived in Egypt out of the reach of Herod. There would always be a demand for carpenters. According to Mark 6:3, the people of Jesus's home town called Jesus 'the carpenter, the son of Mary', which suggests that Joseph had passed on his skills to his son, so that he could provide for the family when Joseph died. Since Jesus didn't leave home until he was thirty, this seems a real possibility.

The people were amazed at Jesus' wisdom and the healing power in his hands, and asked 'where did this man get all this?' (Mark 6:2), as if to say that a carpenter can't have those gifts. But Joseph had spiritual gifts and skilful hands. He was in touch with God and sensitive to his prompting – first when he was told in a dream not to be afraid to take Mary as his wife, and secondly when he was warned in another dream to take his family and flee to Egypt away from the wrath of Herod. Thus his spiritual intuitions saved the young Jesus from a possible early death.

What more, then, could you ask of a father, than a good character, the ability to protect and provide for his wife and family and his willingness to pass on what he knew and believed to his son? Joseph's love to his wife and family showed in these practical ways, and not least in his good example. Whether or not he was Jesus' biological father is neither here nor there and the Bible record doesn't seem to think that matters either. He was a real father to Jesus and as good as any father could be. No wonder then that when Jesus came to speak about his relationship with God he described it in terms of a father and son relationship. God, to him, was always 'Abba' – dad, and if ever Joseph had known that, he would surely have been a proud man. And it was by being a good father, that he was also a good servant of the Lord.

Pause for thought
Do you think that the role of father in the family is more valued today than it has been in the past, or less?

DAY 20
Baby power
Luke 18:15-17

Babies change people's lives. Ask anyone who has just had their first baby and they'll tell you all about it. Life for them has changed completely overnight and it will never be the same again. A new power has entered their home – baby power. Everything revolves around this little bundle of humanity which is now totally dependent on you – for food, warmth, protection, hygiene and love. And it knows instinctively how to get them – it just cries. And when it's not crying, but just lying there waving its arms and legs you can't resist its appeal. To hold it in your arms is a delight, and to see it fast asleep is a delight too. When a baby enters your life you begin to learn the meaning, and the demands, of responsibility and love.

In his book, *The Luck of Roaring Camp*, Bret Harte tells the story of a baby born in a filthy log cabin in the American Wild West. Its mother died in giving birth so it had to be looked after by a gang of rough miners. They wrapped the baby in some dirty rags and put it in a box. But they realised that that didn't look right so they bought a proper cradle. The new cradle made their shack look filthier than ever, so they set to and cleaned it up. They also changed their behaviour. They swore less, drank less, argued less and fought less; and all because of the influence of that helpless little baby.

During Advent we look forward to celebrating the coming of another baby – born in a filthy stable and laid in a feeding trough. The civilising influence of that baby is still being felt throughout the world.

Actually, Advent announces the birth of two babies – John and Jesus, both of whom came at the right time to show people a better way and give them hope of a better life. Neither of them dropped from the sky in a pool of light, like Mr Bean. They came as babies. But that's God's chosen way of changing the world; because most babies grow up and some make a real difference to the way we live, though we don't know that at the time of their birth.

READY FOR CHRISTMAS?

When the Israelites were slaving away in ancient Egypt trying to make bricks out of straw they must have thought that their slavery would last for ever. They didn't know that God had sent a baby, who was lying in a basket in the river Nile; and that baby would grow up to lead them all out of slavery to the promised land.

In AD 680, when most of northern Europe was still pagan, a baby was born in Crediton in Devon, called Wynfrith. He was brought up by Benedictine monks and was fascinated by the stories of visiting missionaries from Germany who told about their attempts to persuade the pagan people to become Christians. At the age of five, Wynfrith decided that when he grew up he wanted to go to Germany himself and tell the people about Jesus. He did just that and, as a priest, and later an archbishop, he was responsible for the conversion of large parts of Europe to the Christian faith, dying a martyr's death in the process. We now know him as St Boniface.

God often works by starting with small things in order to do big things. Tiny seeds become harvests, acorns become oak trees, and eggs which you can only see properly under a microscope, become human beings. That's the kind of world he made, and that's the kind of world to which he sends tiny babies to serve his purposes.

When Queen Victoria visited Michael Faraday in his laboratory to look at some of his work with electricity and magnetism, she asked him what use such studies were. He is said to have replied, 'Madam, of what use is a baby?' Just so.

Pause for thought
What did Jesus mean when he said, 'Whoever does not receive the kingdom of God as a little child will never enter it' (Luke 18:17)?

DAY 21
Great expectations
Luke 2:19, 33-35, 39-40

During Advent we think about two expectant mothers – Elizabeth and Mary. They weren't just expecting babies, they were expecting those babies to grow to be something special. I suppose most mothers think that about their babies in one way or another. Some mothers are so desperate for their children to 'succeed' in life that they push them very hard to achieve success in sport, music, TV, films, theatre or the academic world. In the world of tennis, for instance, we might think of Martina Hingis and her mother.

And fathers can be equally ambitious for their children, illustrated by the success of Tiger Woods in golf and the Williams sisters in tennis. In earlier centuries we have such examples as Mozart and Beethoven, who were both pushed into musical success by their fathers from an early age. Mozart and Beethoven were regarded as child prodigies with exceptional gifts from a very early age. It is as if they had been born to be musicians.

Mozart was once asked by a music student for some advice on writing a concerto, but Mozart said, 'You are too young. Wait until you're a bit older.' The student replied, 'But you composed when you were seven or eight.' 'Yes,' said Mozart, 'but I didn't have to ask anyone how to do it.' Some have to struggle to develop a skill, but others seem to have innate gifts.

We might speculate whether Jesus and John the Baptist were child prodigies. There is certainly a hint of this in the story of Jesus in the Temple, amazing the religious authorities with his knowledge and understanding at the age of twelve (Luke 2:47), but we have no more evidence than that. As for John the Baptist, the angel had told Zechariah that his son would be 'great in the sight of the Lord', and that 'he must never drink wine or strong drink'; and after his birth Luke comments that 'the child grew and became strong in spirit, and he was in the wilderness until the day he appeared publicly to Israel' (Luke 1:80). How old he was when he went into the wilderness we are not told, but it's possible that he was placed in a monastic community by his parents from an early age, perhaps because they were getting too old to care for him themselves.

All that is pure speculation, of course, based on the bare minimum of evidence, but people have always been fascinated by the childhood of people who became famous, and Jesus and John the Baptist are no exceptions to this. I don't know whether there are any imaginative stories about the childhood of John the Baptist, but there are several about the boy Jesus. However, what we know about the two boys is that they both fulfilled their parents' expectations, but, in the case of Jesus at least, not always in a way his mother understood (Luke 2:48-50; Mark 3:20-21, 31-35). Jesus knew that his mission was from God, and only he knew what it meant to fulfil that mission – not his mother or Joseph, but his Father in heaven.

Parents sometimes make the mistake of trying to keep total control of their children's lives, even into adulthood. This used to take the form of making them work down the pit or in the family business. But every individual is unique, with unique gifts, experiences and attitudes, and parents need to be able to guide without undue force or obsessive pressure, to let their offspring eventually let go of their apron strings and find a way in life for themselves. This may mean listening not just to the voice of their parents, but to the deeper authority of a voice within.

We can give Mary the credit for bringing up her son in the way he should go, and then letting him go that way, despite her occasional misgivings, so that when it came to his death, she was still 'there for him' and he was 'there for her' (John 19:25-27).

Pause for thought
Did your parents help you to find your own way in life? Were you able to thank them?

Which of these servants of the Lord can you most identify with – Zechariah, Elizabeth, Mary or Joseph?

DAY 26
Ready?
Luke 1:16-17

At this time of year, the question, 'Are you ready for Christmas?', is often asked, and it's usually meant in a purely secular sense – Have you bought all your presents? Have you sent all your cards? Have you put up your decorations? Have you got in all the food and drink you need? And there is another question too – What are you doing for Christmas? Or we may ask children, 'What do you want for Christmas?' Such questions are all part of the lead up to the Christmas celebration and in the main they are pretty superficial, except that they express a certain communal excitement about the season (though people who are on their own may feel a bit left out by such questions).

But though the questions are trivial enough, the activities they refer to are pretty demanding, so that many people (especially women) get to Christmas day well nigh exhausted, and asking themselves another question, 'Is it really worth it?' So we might well ask ourselves, 'Are the things we are so busy with in the weeks before Christmas anything to do with Christ?'

John the Baptist doesn't feature at all in the commercial Christmas, but he was the one who came 'to make ready a people prepared for the Lord' (Luke 1:17b) and that isn't a question the commercial Christmas is interested in at all. It's not surprising that John the Baptist is lacking in commercial appeal, because he is the exact opposite of that world-wide icon of Christmas commerce – Santa Claus.

Santa lives in a toy factory at the North Pole, a fantasy world of glittering snow. John lives in the heat of the desert, an austere place of hardship and asceticism. Santa wears a bright red suit and has a rosy face and a jolly laugh; and he seems to live on mince pies and glasses of wine. John is clothed in camel's hair and a leather belt. He is a serious preacher, who lives on locusts and wild honey. Santa travels through the air on a sleigh pulled by reindeer to the music of 'Jingle Bells', and visits every house with a sack full of gifts. John comes on foot and invites us to join him in the desert to undergo the baptism of repentance. So there's no contest in the commercial appeal of these two characters. Santa wins hands down every time.

But Santa is pure fantasy; John is reality. Santa offers us everything we want and persuades us that when we've got everything we want, we shall be happy. The result is that we wear ourselves out in the frantic search for the things we want. John points to another who will come to baptise us with the Holy Spirit (Mark 1:8) and will give his own life for the sins of the world (John 1:29). The result is that those who respond receive an energy which enables them to bear spiritual fruit and enter into the kingdom of heaven (Matthew 3:2).

Pause for thought
Who are we most ready for when Christmas comes – Christ, or Santa Claus?

DAY 27
The fruit of repentance
Matthew 3:8; Luke 3:8

John told his hearers to 'bear fruits worthy of repentance'. He said that to the crowd as a whole and to the religious leaders in particular. 'You brood of vipers,' he shouted. 'Who warned you to flee from the wrath to come?' Not words likely to endear him to them, but Jesus didn't always mince his words either (e.g. Matthew 12:34; 23:33).

John warned them not to rely on being descendants of Abraham (any more than we can rely on being descendants of Christians). If they were truly penitent they would show the fruits of it in their lives. We can compare this with what Jesus said to the crowds in the Sermon on the Mount: 'Not everyone who says to me, "Lord, Lord," will enter the kingdom of heaven, but only one who does the will of my Father in heaven. On that day many will say to me, "Lord, Lord, did we not prophesy in your name, and cast out demons in your name, and do many deeds of power in your name?" Then I will declare to them, "I never knew you; go away from me, you evil-doers"' (Matthew 7:21-23).

Uncomfortable words – and not the words we want to hear just before Christmas (or any other time, for that matter). So what are we to make of them? What are the 'fruits worthy of repentance' that John spoke about? Perhaps the crowd were as puzzled as we are, because they came and asked John, 'What then should we do?' (Luke 3:10). John answered by giving instructions to different groups of people (Luke 3:10-14).

Some commentators have regarded John's moral teachings at this point as being rather lightweight, but I don't agree. They are both specific and radical. To the people in general he said, 'Whoever has two coats must share with anyone who has none; and whoever has food must do likewise.' Which of us can honestly say that we literally put that into practice? To the tax collectors John said, 'Collect no more than the amount prescribed for you.' Do *we* always live to that level of honesty? To the soldiers he said, 'Do not extort money from anyone by threats or false accusation, and be satisfied with your wages.' Are *we* never guilty of trying to get what we want by threats and half truths (or downright lies), and who in the world is ever satisfied with their wages?

The genuineness of our repentance is shown not by the words that we say or the rituals that we undertake but by the changes we make in our behaviour. 'What does the Lord require of you,' said the prophet, 'but to do justice, and to love kindness, and to walk humbly with your God?' (Micah 6:8).

John the Baptist is an uncomfortable prophet, telling us things we don't want to hear as well as giving us hopes we hardly dare to believe. But that's what prophets are like, and that's why they provoke opposition and make enemies. People either don't want to hear the truth or they don't believe it – or both. Either way, it means that a prophet's lot is not a happy one (see, for instance, Jeremiah 20:7-10, 14-18), and John doesn't exactly come across as a jolly fellow with a hearty laugh.

However, self-promotion is not John's major purpose – he came to point away from himself to someone greater. 'He himself was not the light, but he came to testify to the light' (John 1:8).

Pause for thought

Jesus says to his followers, 'You are the light of the world . . . Let your light shine before others, so that they may see your good works and give glory to your Father in heaven' (Matthew 5:14a, 16). When we do good are we more conscious of ourselves than we are of the glory of God? How can we avoid that?

DAY 28
The One who is to come
John 1:29-34

A woman went along to a photographic studio to have her picture taken. Haughtily she said to the photographer, 'Young man, make sure you do me justice' but with one look at her face he said, 'It's not justice that you need, madam, it's mercy.' And that's what we all need. As the Psalmist said, 'If you, O Lord, should mark iniquities, Lord, who could stand?' (Psalm 130:3). Justice would destroy us, but mercy saves us.

John the Baptist pointed to Jesus as the one who had come to deal with sin, not by punishing it, but by removing it. In all four Gospels Jesus is distinguished from John the Baptist as the one who will baptise not just with the water of repentance but with the Holy Spirit. Water can wash us outwardly clean for a while, but only the Holy Spirit can make us inwardly new.

Jesus is also distinguished as being not just a prophet but the Son of God (Matthew 3:17; Mark 1:11; Luke 3:22; John 1:34). Only the Son of God can make known the true nature of God (John 1:18) and only the Son of God can bring us the love of God and save us from the just punishment of our sins. (John 3:16-17).

It is only in John's Gospel that the Baptist is said to describe Jesus as 'the Lamb of God who takes away the sin of the world' (John 1:29), but that is undoubtedly how Christians have come to see him. The Lamb of God is the one who offers himself to the world in loving self-sacrifice, first by his mission of love in which he not only taught the supremacy of love, but lived it out to the full; and then by fulfilling his mission through his death on the cross, pouring out his life for the world like the Suffering Servant prophesied in Isaiah 53: 'He was wounded for our transgressions, crushed for our iniquities; upon him was the punishment that made us whole, and by his bruises we are healed.'

So on Christmas Eve we can't help thinking of Holy Week. The shadow of the cross lies over the manger of Bethlehem, for he came in the weakness of love to destroy the power of hate. Paul doesn't record any birth stories about Jesus, but in one famous passage he links Christ's birth with his death in one moving song:

> Though he was in the form of God,
> he did not regard equality with God
> as something to be exploited,
> but emptied himself,
> taking the form of a slave,
> being born in human likeness.
> And being found in human form,
> he humbled himself
> and became obedient
> to the point of death –
> even death on a cross.
> (Philippians 2:6-8)

Love turns enemies into friends. Love forgives sins. Love restores broken lives. Love brings light into the world. Love is the basis of the Law of God. Love reveals the heart of God. So at Christmas time we can rejoice, because, as Christina Georgina Rossetti put it:

> Love came down at Christmas,
> Love all lovely, Love divine;
> Love was born at Christmas,
> star and angels gave the sign.

Pause for thought
Think quietly of the child in the manger. What does it tell you about God's love for the world, and for you?

Biblical Reference Index

OLD TESTAMENT	Day
Genesis 1:1-5	1
Genesis 1:3	1
Genesis 1:5	2
Genesis 18:1-15	15
Genesis 21:1-8	15
Deuteronomy 8:10 (AV)	16
Deuteronomy 15:11	9
Joshua 3	24
1 Samuel 1	15
1 Samuel 2:1-10	18
1 Samuel 2:12	18
1 Samuel 2:21b	18
1 Samuel 3:1	18
1 Samuel 3:13	18
2 Samuel 7:1-11	8
2 Kings 5	24
Job 7:4	4
Psalm 30:5	4
Psalm 37:5 (AV)	16
Psalm 43:3a	2
Psalm 72:1-7	8
Psalm 72:10-11	8
Psalm 72:13-14	8
Psalm 72:18-19	8
Psalm 89:1-4	8
Psalm 89:19-26	8
Psalm 89:46	15
Psalm 118:27a	7
Psalm 119:72, 103	8
Psalm 119:105	7, 8

OLD TESTAMENT	Day
Psalm 130:1, 6	5
Psalm 130:3	28
Proverbs 29:18 (AV)	18
Isaiah 2:1-5	8
Isaiah 2:4	10
Isaiah 6:8	17
Isaiah 9:2	5, 8
Isaiah 9:2-7	8
Isaiah 9:6-7	5
Isaiah 11:1-10	8
Isaiah 42:4	9
Isaiah 43:18-19a	13
Isaiah 43:25	16
Isaiah 49:6	8
Isaiah 49:15	16
Isaiah 53	28
Isaiah 61:1-2a	18
Isaiah 64:4	3
Jeremiah 20:7-10	27
Jeremiah 20:14-18	27
Jeremiah 29:11	8
Jeremiah 31:34	16
Lamentations 3:22-24	4
Daniel 7:13-15	13
Amos 5:24	9
Micah 4:3	10
Micah 5:1-5a	8
Micah 6:8	27
Malachi 4:5	15, 22
Malachi 4:6	15

NEW TESTAMENT	Day	NEW TESTAMENT	Day
Matthew 1:1-16	19	Mark 3:20-21	21
Matthew 1:18-25	19	Mark 3:31-35	21
Matthew 1:19	19	Mark 6:2	19
Matthew 1:20	19	Mark 6:3	19
Matthew 3:2	24, 26	Mark 13	11
Matthew 3:2, 5-6	24	Mark 13:7-8	11
Matthew 3:7	24	Mark 13:13b	11
Matthew 3:8	27	Mark 13:22	11
Matthew 3:12	24	Mark 13:32	11
Matthew 3:17	28	Luke 1:5-25	15
Matthew 4:17	24	Luke 1:6	15
Matthew 5:14a, 16	12, 27	Luke 1:13b	15
Matthew 7:21-23	27	Luke 1:16-17	26
Matthew 7:24-27	13	Luke 1:17	15
Matthew 8:10	17	Luke 1:17b	15, 26
Matthew 11:2-3	24	Luke 1:26-38	17
Matthew 11:4-6	24	Luke 1:32-33, 69	8
Matthew 11:7-15	24	Luke 1:38	17
Matthew 11:11	24	Luke 1:39-45	15
Matthew 12:34	27	Luke 1:46-55	8, 18
Matthew 13:55	19	Luke 1:50-54	8
Matthew 13:58	17	Luke 1:57-80	15
Matthew 17:17	17	Luke 1:79	8
Matthew 17:20	17	Luke 1:80	21
Matthew 19:26	9	Luke 2:4	19
Matthew 23:33	27	Luke 2:19	21
Matthew 24	11	Luke 2:21	19
Matthew 24:6	10, 11	Luke 2:22-24	19
Matthew 24:7	11	Luke 2:32	8
Matthew 24:13	11	Luke 2:33-35	21
Matthew 24:24	11	Luke 2:39-40	21
Matthew 24:46	11	Luke 2:41	19
Matthew 25:31-46	25	Luke 2:47	21
Matthew 26:11	9	Luke 2:48-50	21
Mark 1:4-5	23	Luke 2:52	18
Mark 1:8	26	Luke 3:8	27
Mark 1:11	28	Luke 3:10	27
Mark 1:15	12, 24	Luke 3:10-14	27

DAY 26
Ready? Luke 1:16-17

At this time of year, the question, 'Are you ready for Christmas?', is often asked, and it's usually meant in a purely secular sense – Have you bought all your presents? Have you sent all your cards? Have you put up your decorations? Have you got in all the food and drink you need? And there is another question too – What are you doing for Christmas? Or we may ask children, 'What do you want for Christmas?' Such questions are all part of the lead up to the Christmas celebration and in the main they are pretty superficial, except that they express a certain communal excitement about the season (though people who are on their own may feel a bit left out by such questions).

But though the questions are trivial enough, the activities they refer to are pretty demanding, so that many people (especially women) get to Christmas day well nigh exhausted, and asking themselves another question, 'Is it really worth it?' So we might well ask ourselves, 'Are the things we are so busy with in the weeks before Christmas anything to do with Christ?'

John the Baptist doesn't feature at all in the commercial Christmas, but he was the one who came 'to make ready a people prepared for the Lord' (Luke 1:17b) and that isn't a question the commercial Christmas is interested in at all. It's not surprising that John the Baptist is lacking in commercial appeal, because he is the exact opposite of that world-wide icon of Christmas commerce – Santa Claus.

Santa lives in a toy factory at the North Pole, a fantasy world of glittering snow. John lives in the heat of the desert, an austere place of hardship and asceticism. Santa wears a bright red suit and has a rosy face and a jolly laugh; and he seems to live on mince pies and glasses of wine. John is clothed in camel's hair and a leather belt. He is a serious preacher, who lives on locusts and wild honey. Santa travels through the air on a sleigh pulled by reindeer to the music of 'Jingle Bells', and visits every house with a sack full of gifts. John comes on foot and invites us to join him in the desert to undergo the baptism of repentance. So there's no contest in the commercial appeal of these two characters. Santa wins hands down every time.

But Santa is pure fantasy; John is reality. Santa offers us everything we want and persuades us that when we've got everything we want, we shall be happy. The result is that we wear ourselves out in the frantic search for the things we want. John points to another who will come to baptise us with the Holy Spirit (Mark 1:8) and will give his own life for the sins of the world (John 1:29). The result is that those who respond receive an energy which enables them to bear spiritual fruit and enter into the kingdom of heaven (Matthew 3:2).

Pause for thought
Who are we most ready for when Christmas comes – Christ, or Santa Claus?

DAY 27
The fruit of repentance
Matthew 3:8; Luke 3:8

John told his hearers to 'bear fruits worthy of repentance'. He said that to the crowd as a whole and to the religious leaders in particular. 'You brood of vipers,' he shouted. 'Who warned you to flee from the wrath to come?' Not words likely to endear him to them, but Jesus didn't always mince his words either (e.g. Matthew 12:34; 23:33).

John warned them not to rely on being descendants of Abraham (any more than we can rely on being descendants of Christians). If they were truly penitent they would show the fruits of it in their lives. We can compare this with what Jesus said to the crowds in the Sermon on the Mount: 'Not everyone who says to me, "Lord, Lord," will enter the kingdom of heaven, but only one who does the will of my Father in heaven. On that day many will say to me, "Lord, Lord, did we not prophesy in your name, and cast out demons in your name, and do many deeds of power in your name?" Then I will declare to them, "I never knew you; go away from me, you evil-doers"' (Matthew 7:21-23).

Uncomfortable words – and not the words we want to hear just before Christmas (or any other time, for that matter). So what are we to make of them? What are the 'fruits worthy of repentance' that John spoke about? Perhaps the crowd were as puzzled as we are, because they came and asked John, 'What then should we do?' (Luke 3:10). John answered by giving instructions to different groups of people (Luke 3:10-14).

Some commentators have regarded John's moral teachings at this point as being rather lightweight, but I don't agree. They are both specific and radical. To the people in general he said, 'Whoever has two coats must share with anyone who has none; and whoever has food must do likewise.' Which of us can honestly say that we literally put that into practice? To the tax collectors John said, 'Collect no more than the amount prescribed for you.' Do *we* always live to that level of honesty? To the soldiers he said, 'Do not extort money from anyone by threats or false accusation, and be satisfied with your wages.' Are *we* never guilty of trying to get what we want by threats and half truths (or downright lies), and who in the world is ever satisfied with their wages?

The genuineness of our repentance is shown not by the words that we say or the rituals that we undertake but by the changes we make in our behaviour. 'What does the Lord require of you,' said the prophet, 'but to do justice, and to love kindness, and to walk humbly with your God?' (Micah 6:8).

John the Baptist is an uncomfortable prophet, telling us things we don't want to hear as well as giving us hopes we hardly dare to believe. But that's what prophets are like, and that's why they provoke opposition and make enemies. People either don't want to hear the truth or they don't believe it – or both. Either way, it means that a prophet's lot is not a happy one (see, for instance, Jeremiah 20:7-10, 14-18), and John doesn't exactly come across as a jolly fellow with a hearty laugh.

However, self-promotion is not John's major purpose – he came to point away from himself to someone greater. 'He himself was not the light, but he came to testify to the light' (John 1:8).

Pause for thought
Jesus says to his followers, 'You are the light of the world . . . Let your light shine before others, so that they may see your good works and give glory to your Father in heaven' (Matthew 5:14a, 16). When we do good are we more conscious of ourselves than we are of the glory of God? How can we avoid that?

DAY 28
The One who is to come
John 1:29-34

A woman went along to a photographic studio to have her picture taken. Haughtily she said to the photographer, 'Young man, make sure you do me justice' but with one look at her face he said, 'It's not justice that you need, madam, it's mercy.' And that's what we all need. As the Psalmist said, 'If you, O Lord, should mark iniquities, Lord, who could stand?' (Psalm 130:3). Justice would destroy us, but mercy saves us.

John the Baptist pointed to Jesus as the one who had come to deal with sin, not by punishing it, but by removing it. In all four Gospels Jesus is distinguished from John the Baptist as the one who will baptise not just with the water of repentance but with the Holy Spirit. Water can wash us outwardly clean for a while, but only the Holy Spirit can make us inwardly new.

Jesus is also distinguished as being not just a prophet but the Son of God (Matthew 3:17; Mark 1:11; Luke 3:22; John 1:34). Only the Son of God can make known the true nature of God (John 1:18) and only the Son of God can bring us the love of God and save us from the just punishment of our sins. (John 3:16-17).

It is only in John's Gospel that the Baptist is said to describe Jesus as 'the Lamb of God who takes away the sin of the world' (John 1:29), but that is undoubtedly how Christians have come to see him. The Lamb of God is the one who offers himself to the world in loving self-sacrifice, first by his mission of love in which he not only taught the supremacy of love, but lived it out to the full; and then by fulfilling his mission through his death on the cross, pouring out his life for the world like the Suffering Servant prophesied in Isaiah 53: 'He was wounded for our transgressions, crushed for our iniquities; upon him was the punishment that made us whole, and by his bruises we are healed.'

So on Christmas Eve we can't help thinking of Holy Week. The shadow of the cross lies over the manger of Bethlehem, for he came in the weakness of love to destroy the power of hate. Paul doesn't record any birth stories about Jesus, but in one famous passage he links Christ's birth with his death in one moving song:

> Though he was in the form of God,
> he did not regard equality with God
> as something to be exploited,
> but emptied himself,
> taking the form of a slave,
> being born in human likeness.
> And being found in human form,
> he humbled himself
> and became obedient
> to the point of death –
> even death on a cross.
>
> (Philippians 2:6-8)

Love turns enemies into friends. Love forgives sins. Love restores broken lives. Love brings light into the world. Love is the basis of the Law of God. Love reveals the heart of God. So at Christmas time we can rejoice, because, as Christina Georgina Rossetti put it:

> Love came down at Christmas,
> Love all lovely, Love divine;
> Love was born at Christmas,
> star and angels gave the sign.

Pause for thought
Think quietly of the child in the manger. What does it tell you about God's love for the world, and for you?

Biblical Reference Index

OLD TESTAMENT	Day	OLD TESTAMENT	Day
Genesis 1:1-5	1	Psalm 130:1, 6	5
Genesis 1:3	1	Psalm 130:3	28
Genesis 1:5	2	Proverbs 29:18 (AV)	18
Genesis 18:1-15	15	Isaiah 2:1-5	8
Genesis 21:1-8	15	Isaiah 2:4	10
Deuteronomy 8:10 (AV)	16	Isaiah 6:8	17
Deuteronomy 15:11	9	Isaiah 9:2	5, 8
Joshua 3	24	Isaiah 9:2-7	8
1 Samuel 1	15	Isaiah 9:6-7	5
1 Samuel 2:1-10	18	Isaiah 11:1-10	8
1 Samuel 2:12	18	Isaiah 42:4	9
1 Samuel 2:21b	18	Isaiah 43:18-19a	13
1 Samuel 3:1	18	Isaiah 43:25	16
1 Samuel 3:13	18	Isaiah 49:6	8
2 Samuel 7:1-11	8	Isaiah 49:15	16
2 Kings 5	24	Isaiah 53	28
Job 7:4	4	Isaiah 61:1-2a	18
Psalm 30:5	4	Isaiah 64:4	3
Psalm 37:5 (AV)	16	Jeremiah 20:7-10	27
Psalm 43:3a	2	Jeremiah 20:14-18	27
Psalm 72:1-7	8	Jeremiah 29:11	8
Psalm 72:10-11	8	Jeremiah 31:34	16
Psalm 72:13-14	8	Lamentations 3:22-24	4
Psalm 72:18-19	8	Daniel 7:13-15	13
Psalm 89:1-4	8	Amos 5:24	9
Psalm 89:19-26	8	Micah 4:3	10
Psalm 89:46	15	Micah 5:1-5a	8
Psalm 118:27a	7	Micah 6:8	27
Psalm 119:72, 103	8	Malachi 4:5	15, 22
Psalm 119:105	7, 8	Malachi 4:6	15

67

NEW TESTAMENT	Day	NEW TESTAMENT	Day
Matthew 1:1-16	19	Mark 3:20-21	21
Matthew 1:18-25	19	Mark 3:31-35	21
Matthew 1:19	19	Mark 6:2	19
Matthew 1:20	19	Mark 6:3	19
Matthew 3:2	24, 26	Mark 13	11
Matthew 3:2, 5-6	24	Mark 13:7-8	11
Matthew 3:7	24	Mark 13:13b	11
Matthew 3:8	27	Mark 13:22	11
Matthew 3:12	24	Mark 13:32	11
Matthew 3:17	28	Luke 1:5-25	15
Matthew 4:17	24	Luke 1:6	15
Matthew 5:14a, 16	12, 27	Luke 1:13b	15
Matthew 7:21-23	27	Luke 1:16-17	26
Matthew 7:24-27	13	Luke 1:17	15
Matthew 8:10	17	Luke 1:17b	15, 26
Matthew 11:2-3	24	Luke 1:26-38	17
Matthew 11:4-6	24	Luke 1:32-33, 69	8
Matthew 11:7-15	24	Luke 1:38	17
Matthew 11:11	24	Luke 1:39-45	15
Matthew 12:34	27	Luke 1:46-55	8, 18
Matthew 13:55	19	Luke 1:50-54	8
Matthew 13:58	17	Luke 1:57-80	15
Matthew 17:17	17	Luke 1:79	8
Matthew 17:20	17	Luke 1:80	21
Matthew 19:26	9	Luke 2:4	19
Matthew 23:33	27	Luke 2:19	21
Matthew 24	11	Luke 2:21	19
Matthew 24:6	10, 11	Luke 2:22-24	19
Matthew 24:7	11	Luke 2:32	8
Matthew 24:13	11	Luke 2:33-35	21
Matthew 24:24	11	Luke 2:39-40	21
Matthew 24:46	11	Luke 2:41	19
Matthew 25:31-46	25	Luke 2:47	21
Matthew 26:11	9	Luke 2:48-50	21
Mark 1:4-5	23	Luke 2:52	18
Mark 1:8	26	Luke 3:8	27
Mark 1:11	28	Luke 3:10	27
Mark 1:15	12, 24	Luke 3:10-14	27

BIBLICAL REFERENCE INDEX

NEW TESTAMENT	Day	NEW TESTAMENT	Day
Luke 3:22	28	John 3:19-21	25
Luke 3:23-38	19	John 19:25-27	21
Luke 4:16	19	Acts 9:3-9	6
Luke 4:21	18	Acts 14:22	11
Luke 10:9	12	Romans 8:38-39	11
Luke 11:20	12	Romans 12:17, 21	14
Luke 18:15-17	20	Romans 13:12	12
Luke 18:17	20	1 Corinthians 2:9-10a	3
Luke 19:41-46	19	1 Corinthians 3:5-9	16
Luke 21:9, 11-12, 25	11	2 Corinthians 4:8	1
Luke 21:25-36	11	2 Corinthians 4:18	3
Luke 21:27	13	2 Corinthians 5:7	3
John 1:8	27	Philippians 2:6-8	28
John 1:18	28	2 Timothy 4:2 (AV)	16
John 1:29	26, 28	Hebrews 11:1-3	3
John 1:29-34	28	2 Peter 3:8	16
John 1:34	28	2 Peter 3:9	16
John 3:16-17	28	1 John 1:5	1, 3
John 3:17	25	Revelation 21:23-24	1